small flames

small flames

Dina E. Cox

George Payerle, Editor

Second printing, 2013

Cover design by Doowah Design.
Photo of Dina Cox by Roger Carlsen Photography.

Printed and bound in Canada by M&T Printing.

We acknowledge the support of The Canada Council for the Arts and the Manitoba Arts Council for our publishing program.

Library and Archives Canada Cataloguing in Publication

Cox, Dina E., 1946–
Small flames / Dina E. Cox.

Poems.
ISBN 978-1-897109-92-2

I. Title.

PS8605.O9352S63 2012 C811'.6 C2012-901731-0

Signature Editions
P.O. Box 206, RPO Corydon, Winnipeg, Manitoba, R3M 3S7
www.signature-editions.com

in memory of my parents

Beryl Carter and Gordon Ernest Coates

with gratitude and love always

CONTENTS

GEOGRAPHIES

KADDISH

DIVERTIMENTO

LEGACIES

GEOGRAPHIES

Saint John Childhood

Growing up on Orange Street
we cut the weed-choked grass
with a sickle,
celebrated the arrival of
our first wringer washer —
wet clothes soon flapping
on the line — and hoisted
bags of coal four storeys
to our flat's coldroom to stow
then burn the winter long,
cleaning daily
to erase thick layers
of black dust that seeped
into our lives from the depths
of mines in Nova Scotia.

At night through open casements
the salt-soaked harbour air
infused each pore with dampness
while from beyond the breakwater
the soft *ooh-ah* of a foghorn
comforted
and sleep came easily.

Morning's sun brought
games of marbles,
stubby fingers scratching
circles in cinders, risking
all before we moved on
to hopscotch and red rover,
or rushed with sweaty palms
and pennies to the Pitt Stop
for licorice sticks and bubble gum

then tumbled out again, laughter
roiling on the brine-filled air,
shouts of joy and seagulls
indistinguishable.

Walking the Eston Hills for the First Time

Oh Eston Hills! Home of the root of me
where gorse and heather converge
seamlessly, once warder of the ironstone
your rich veins promised, your pulse
yet throbs with blood of those who'd thought
to profit from your hard won ore.

I look at you now, *Cnaep*, Nab over Eston
foreign to my tongue and yet familiar,
adorned with charms to bedevil suitors,
marked by wayfarers who leave their footprints
as fair exchange for what's more lasting,
a page of history gleaned from the core
of you, absorbed by osmosis, filling
my empty spaces this late summer afternoon.

Today your green and shadowed slopes
lie silent save for the piercing jackdaws
black as coal, black as iron — black as memory,
as the faces of miners thrust suddenly
into sunlight from the earth's dark vaults,
their dust-laden lungs gasping
for air, as mine do today from this climb

but not from this climb only… dear hills
where I am rooted, even before sentience
you left your mark in me, and all this while
you were only waiting to reclaim your own.

In Westminster Abbey

I touched Chaucer's tomb six hundred years
after he was laid to rest (though not at first
in it), its marble surface cool to my outstretched
hand still warm from the late summer's lazy sun.

Here inside the cavernous Abbey — Chaucer,
spinner of yarns, Clerk of the King's Works;
he lies, not with flesh but among those
now dust, whose words have sung to me
their intractable songs, preserved
in the chill, unyielding spaces of the Abbey,
entombed in imagined memory, their bodies
wizened relics of what was once human,
obedient to nature and to that which holds them.

I touched Chaucer's voiceless tomb,
guardian of what remains, yet unable
to contain the whispers of poems that rustle
like the unfettered wings of angels, having
no longer any business with grave things.

Geographies

The bastion cliff at Saltburn-by-the-Sea
stands boldly east-nor'-east for Frisia and
it resembles a PEI promontory, flat-topped,
planted with patchwork grasses   some farmer's
summer's diligence — its craggy reach eroded,
it might be a puzzle piece waiting to be fitted
just so, looking to complete itself

and in my mind I search for and find Cape Tryon,
north shore, red sandstone, mounting a fierce resistance
to the determined Atlantic rollers, and I'm tempted
to edge them together, cusp and cup,
but it doesn't work.
I remember Cape Tryon looks
only towards Quebec, does not stretch
across an ocean, and yet the thought is so clear,
the semblance of conjunction so real, if only
for a moment; and thus imagination plays
its game, making illusions of dreams,
sometimes even of what we'd thought to touch.

Cape Tryon, PEI

The necks of cormorants undulate
in silence over the late-afternoon cliffs
of Cape Tryon, sound of their wings
drowned in the constant surge of ocean;

a small squadron of them rises
darkly from their sandstone bastion,
oblivious to the bipedal trespassers
who inch gingerly along the cliff's edge,
winding awkwardly through the tall
wind blown grasses of the promontory.

This place is like a child's unschooled
drawing, bold with the wash of sea spray,
blue with the depths of sky and ocean.
The Permian redbeds, sharply defined,
extend their stolid bulk into the sparkling
waters, and over all, the fluid blackness
of incurious birds scaling Aeolian currents,
themselves possessed by the spirits of mariners
returned from the edge of an ancient world
to claim what is theirs.

Crayola Moon

The balloon moon hangs heavy
just grazing   the horizon
tipping trees as if
some child had taken crayons,
chosen mango orange and outlined
a three-quarters orb
then filled it in,
having no need
to draw the whole.

Old Barn

for David McKay

walking inside
you are surrounded
by silence, the kind
that wraps itself
around you in a snow storm
where nothing else exists
but you and the warm whiteness
of snow; minutes pass and then

voices, their soft murmur a tonic
story of cows no longer there
but you can feel them, feel
the wetness of thick tongues,
their warm breath, their curious
staring as they follow your steps
in the packed straw, heavy
with the smell of cow but
no steam rising from fresh pats;

still you can tell something
lingers in the air you inhale,
in the echo of empty stalls,
in the feeling you are not alone,
in the almost-sour scent of
spilled milk and the remembered
swish of bovine tails, flies
being constant — even today

flies slap indolently
at window panes. Long after
the last milk cans clattered trucks
to city markets, flies maintain
their reassuring provocation…

on the window's ledge, dust,
so thick you could scoop
handfuls, rub it between
uncalloused palms, lift it
to breathe deeply stories
of other days, but you don't,
you choose not to disturb
that fragrant legacy...

flailing the gelid light
the bluebottles' dissonance
is the only actual sound
as you stand unmoving
as you try to read meaning
into the moment, as you wish
for just one winter spider
to parachute from rotting rafters
through the pallid sun's rays,
its thread somehow proof
of your own tenuous hold
on life

Apple

In my hand an apple, store-bought.
Here, take it, hold out your palm
and feel its weight, how it presses
your lifeline, rolls over it,   of course

the apple you hold is not an apple
of summer growing fatter daily,
soaking up sun and sucking rain
where it attaches surely to its

weighted branch, and it is definitely
not autumn-ripe or round-luscious
tempting you to sink your teeth greedily
into its tart juices. It will not set them

on edge or spurt its sudden sweetness
onto your eager tongue, nor will it
convey the seductive ardour of sunshine,
the urgent imperative of wind or rain,

the lingering dankness of earth. Still
it's a good apple for all that, even
desirable in its ordinary way, but

it's not the sort of apple young boys
pluck to flatter earnest teachers or
bite heartily just because it's there
no matter on which side of the fence —

you'd need to pick it fresh off the tree
for that, textured temptation, shining,
more than a young lad can resist.

small flames

their tongues
leap for air, all of it hot
in the untouchable dome
that marks the campfire's
reach; from luminous coals
they rise looking to devour
whatever they can find,
birch bark, driftwood and
the rapt attention of those
who warm body parts against
night's advancing chill...

escaping dreams in ochre,
a chartreuse thought, an idea
growing out of crimson lace
and purple canyons, the way
light teases sight, confounds
what we see with what we think
we see, and the cerulean depths
of sky, hypnotizing, drawing
all that is into itself for the
longest fraction of a moment;

a sun-warmed field of lupins
burns as brightly, peppering
the transparent air with pungent
colour, each stalk stretching
joyfully like fingers reaching
towards some attainable goal
before the capricious breeze
turns and plashes them anew
so that a passing artist paints
their essence only, the canvas
a wild involvement, its timbre
incendiary, seething

Toogood Pond

Cicada's song in the rising heat
of morning, and a woodpecker choosing
not to peck the bleached trunk of a nameless
tree, and all the nameless trees that arch
the boardwalk and the river before it joins
the pond; they might be willows or elms
or ashes or birches but it is no matter,
nature's *chupa* as far as the eye can see
perhaps into eternity, and from it the cries
of redwings and in the distance a haunting
cry of crow;

the reflections of those wooden arms become
one with the waters below, and there
the still form of a bird, but not a bird,
a small piece of deadwood poised on the
likeness of a branch, so still the water,

stiller the leaves that weave their dense
canopy against the seamless blue of sky,
and all is breathless as if even the moment
itself were out of time save for the cicada;

I remember the day is Sabbath, all one
to the creatures whose world I have invaded,
but here under the spreading arms that hold
me fast, chorused by the susurrant rhythms
of day's awakening, I am moved to whisper
reverently, *Selah*.

Command Performance

I'd been looking for a poem all week, trying to come up with something of import, something meaningful, finally giving up, putting on the coffee, bringing my mug out to the front stoop, then sitting there to overlook the bay where the tide was slowly ebbing and the still-blue sky stood like a painted backdrop for the local high school's staged operetta, where the actors foiled by that clear sky were clapboard houses, front and centre, no two the same colour, like costumes in a Gilbert and Sullivan chorus, yellow, cream, light grey, pea-green, slate grey and brown, each house marching down the hill, each close enough above the other to be like stairs rising or descending, and above all the dark flat roofs (for I sat on my stoop higher than all) the bay sprawled unabashed in sunshine, its waters calm, a painted scene under the blue-domed sky with only me to ponder how all this could have been staged for me alone.

Two Small Poems from Virgin Gorda

I

The dipper hangs low
    to the horizon,
leaning
into a black ocean
or seeming to;
            perhaps
it only wants a moment
to scoop the dark stars
and lift them, shimmering,
back into the heavens.

II

On First Seeing a Turk's Cap Cactus

Your virility dependent
on a few inches
of rain every year
                    I'm glad
I did not come upon you
in a dry season.

KADDISH

What We Want

What we want, what we
can't have flies past reason

like a sparrow eyeing
the crumb I dropped just
now; it won't venture
under my foot, finds
another way.

I see no fear but my own
that tells me what I can't have,
draws invisible lines;
                                        you see
only a slight tightening
of my mouth.

The sparrow returns again
and again, remembering
sweetness.

A gentle breeze stirs.
I see only the sparrow
and a memory of crumbs.

Diagnosis

Limned with hoar frost
an alien geography
speeds past car windows

arms frozen in supplication
skeletal trees incandesce

as a lingering half-moon
fades into the white-blue

sky; this is the day a doctor
will name the unusual gestures
a small boy makes

The naming will stick
long after moon's demise
after a cold sun dissolves
the rimy whiteness
into air

A Palpable Confluency

"You have a palpable confluency"
the doctor says quietly, steadily,
and I watch as my own hand
follows his, moves to find it,
touches the outer upper left
quadrant numbly, feeling for nothing
finding something   palpable
just what he'd said. I press gently
and its substance surprises me,
I wince, breathe in sharply.

Later a friend tells me "If it hurts
it can't be cancer" offering hope,
her own voiceless cancer so
recently excised;
I'm grasping
but I don't know what to do
what to think, whether I can
hope it away, this uninvited
guest at my table, my own
palpable reality.

The Gift

I

It might be
in this moment,
my father in X-ray,
that the biopsy needle
pierces his skin,
the young doctor
guiding it through
dermis and epidermis,
through layers of weakened muscle
to penetrate the pleural sac, intent
on its course, that irregular nodule
"just two-and-a-half centimetres"

just two-and-a-half centimetres
and a steady hand standing
between knowing
and not knowing

II

Diagnosis: cancer —
yet the gift of more
than the allotted
three score and ten
can not dull the edge
of this pervasive sadness;
still, my father observes
that now we *know*
what we are dealing with…

III

After the doctor leaves
I search for something
concrete to hold onto:
in silence I soap each
of my father's leathered soles,
awed by the intimacy
of fingers and toes,
and by his acceptance
of this macabre dance.

A Lesson in Geometry

gaunt
you are all angles,
a theorem in geometry
awaiting solution

in a right angle triangle
the sum of the squares
on the sides which form
the right angle
equals the square
on the hypotenuse...

I watch as you shift
your legs, deliberately
as if they were not
yours, and I see

there are no *right*
angles here
only those
of jutting chin,
of cheekbone pushing
against yellowed skin
and the sorry-sad

angle of light your eyes
level at me
not daring to whisper
the question that hangs
between us, connecting
all the angles,

and you,
becoming one
with that right angle,
disappearing into it,
confined by
an unyielding hypotenuse —

the solution
is all wrong,

and there is no
escape, only
the frailty of skin
sinking into itself

and this stubborn angle
of bone

Return Flight

I

waiting
among strangers
having cleared
security
                checking
to be sure of what
I did not bring

wondering if the efficient
X-ray machine also
caught the metallic pain
of me leaving
my dying father

II

neither here nor there
but 28,000 feet above
the bed you lie on
wishing for my return
                                I imagine
how you shift in pain
on an institutional mattress
and, like a child beginning
a too-long journey, sigh
and ask silent walls
how long before
you get there

Dementia

moving day
hoping he'll like
the nursing home,
already he forgets
where he is

arguing
with my father
over details
he no longer remembers
but I cannot forget

necessity is
an indwelling catheter
no need to pee…
still he forgets and
shuffles to the bathroom

we listen
to Domingo's *Perhaps Love*
his favourite,
he looks at the stereo,
asks anxiously *What's that?*

Where's Mum?
he asks softly,
I hesitate too long…
my father doesn't remember
she's gone

after my visit
he promptly forgets
I was there,
trapped in each passing moment
he steals even my memories

will I live
long enough to write
of this sadness —
some days I fear I will live
long enough to know it

in silence
cherry blossoms
fall softly,
in his growing darkness
my father listens

Daddy's Last Dance

five years ago
I watched you dance
at a wedding
arthritic knees forgotten

you, jiving in your light grey checked suit
you, filled with the wine of a different day

today I watch
as you struggle
to breathe,
bony fingers curled
round the metal bedrail,
your body strewn with
plastic tubing,
and I want to shout

Dance Daddy dance!
as fast as you can…
arise like Lazarus,
shake off this
dead man's shuffle
and savour life
one last time

even if it must take you
away from me…

but your scuffed slippers
remain unmoving
under the bed

After visiting my father in the nursing home

his 'privates' no longer
private — subject of much
discussion, closely
scrutinized, no longer
desired, only desiring
to function normally,
                    and the indignity
of catheterization which
does the job yet fails
to eliminate the urgency,
the incessant burning
and the convergence of
every thought where once
pleasure arose, now defined
only by pain
                    and he
must speak of it
to whomever will listen
and offer him
some small measure
of pity

In My Father's House

There are no more photos
to take, I've taken them all

from every angle
inside and out
living room
dining room
basement, wherever
sentiment commands
                    even
the piano he bought me
hoisting it four stories
by pulley to the old flat,
his second hand expression
of first hand love
              moved finally
to this house.

From the neglected hutch
I line up aimless rows
of teacups, the fancy ones
kept only for company,
                    line them up
and start shooting again,
capturing Aynsley scrolls and
Royal Albert roses on cups
whose rims no longer know
the polite sip of graciousness,
the heated kiss of high tea,
the gentle clinking
of spoons, and then
                    done,

replace them, carefully,
as if they might yet find purpose,
as if nothing had changed
as if I still lived here
as if this were not
somehow necessary.

Liturgy of the Last Days

"Have you told Mum you're here?"
My mother died twenty years ago.

"Where's Mummy? Where's Daddy?"
His parents died before I was born.

"It isn't good not to eat anything."
Here Daddy, try just one bite…

"No…, no…, I feel sick."
Maybe if you eat something…

"It isn't good that a person lie in bed all day."
I know Daddy, I know.

"I've got to get UP!"
Maybe later, when you're feeling stronger.

"This too shall pass."
Yes Daddy, you've always said that.

"I want to go home, to Heaven."
I'm sure that's where you'll go, but maybe not today.

"Water… water."

"Hurts… hurts."

"There are no daughters… there are no daughters."

After a Funeral

for Mary Cox, my mother-in-law

the house where death has entered
                    is quiet
                    is noisy

too many voices
too many whispers
accusing
          not yet
comforting

the sweet smell
of wilting chrysanthemums
accosts...

                    what you did
                    what you did not do

handwritten cards hold
their studied distance
as sunlight tracks new dust
across unchanged mahogany

from the kitchen
where words are not spoken,
an odour of dinner turned low
and the silence
of a widow
still unsure
how to wear
her new clothes

His Felt Cap

Between monitor and keyboard it rests lightly
on my *Oxford New Thesaurus for the 1990s*,
wordless for all that, his felt camel-coloured cap.

Some might deem it shabby yet it musters
the shape of his head, how it crowned, tilted;
I remember that he wore it jauntily, askew.

Thus it sat on the head of such a man, my father —
serious, worried, perfunctory, a man who gave
commands, expected results.
                                        How many times
it warmed his head, taking shape from his particular
synthesis of bone, hair and grey matter... aged
in the swirl of cigarette smoke and a widower's portion.

On his seventy-fifth birthday we went to Market
bought cheese, breathed deeply past stands of dulse
(quietly remembering
my mother's love of it)
and freshly harvested seafood, swallowing
the old salt aroma of primal spawning grounds...

Finally we found the soft ice cream stand.
A peacock strutting, he made much of choosing
from 24 flavours, my father who never enjoyed shopping
now playing at it with his only daughter.

A benediction borrowed from ancient cathedrals,
light found his cap, settled on it, transformed it.
I remember how he came alive for me that day,
his felt cap drawing rays to itself
as the sun draws water.

In My Imagination

for J.S. 1945-2006

I imagine your room,
the big window facing south,
the cold brightness
of winter opening up,
the bed you adjust yourself

I imagine friends
family and others
visiting you,
palliative care workers
keeping the background

This is the room
where you will die,
it is not home
but you are surrounded
by love; I imagine

your morphined mind
looking for a balance,
groggy, your mind
that was always exact,
your ready wit

I imagine you
in that homely room
become the paradox
as you always did — grateful,
still asking the questions

I cannot imagine
a world without you,
focus instead
on that window facing south,
imagine you asking someone

to open it

Closed Doors

for my friend Pam

My mother remembers no more.
Giver of life and love
she no longer grasps the meaning
of former goals and purposes,
of hopes and dreams.
Lost in a diminishing world
she can no longer connect
the dots of friends and family
nor understand why
they should even be connected.
Only in brief moments
does her mind's eye see —
and then her pain and frustration
are more than I can bear.

Memories overwhelm,
breaking through the sculpted
veneer of my life, forcing me
to accept this progression
from what was once
to what is now,
and what is to come,
closing
the door against her future
forever.

I have become my mother's mother.
I want to say "I'm sorry for
your pain, I love you Mum," and
"Thank you for your great gift
of love."
I only hold her close.

Covering her hand with mine
I tell her it will be okay,
blink hard against this reality
that is both hers and mine...
the memories of this moment
that are mine
                    alone

Kaddish

I

Once after she died
I stood at the edge
of her kitchen and

she moved me, made me
move my legs to cross it
one more time,

then my mother was gone
forever.
        I can still feel
my legs moving, not
of their own volition.

II

After my father died,
the warmth of his hand
in mine, I sat beside him
for a long while, just sat
there, and it was enough.

Orphaned, I shook
hands with the stranger
I had become, and so
prepared myself for
the rest of my life.

III

In the beginning the Word
became flesh.
Now only words remain.

I imagine their souls
as I search to name

the faces of memory,
to illumine
the language of my dead.

DIVERTIMENTO

Horn

Against black velvet
the gold of its coils
shines brilliantly —
my horn's song is perfect
as long as it's in the case.

One might not guess
the snake's power,
coiled in sleep,
like a child full of dreams
whose limp limbs slumber on.

Once
a small child loved
the smell of crayons —
grown, that same child inhales
slide grease and valve oil.

The cold of metal,
its weight in my hands,
its silence —
I feel like a god, my breath
warming it, giving it life.

At my touch
metal softens,
sings —

I'd like to think
its song rises soulfully

as valves push
against fingers
and lips seek
their place of flawless
symphysis.

Reality is
there is no uncoiling,
only tension,
as I measure horn's timbre
note by note.

After the Music

after the music
empty tables
line the street

hot café mocha
in the breeze a hint
of autumn

Sunday morning:
a parade of SUVs
stirs the dust

it's early yet —
only one familiar face
in the village

sunless sky,
echoes of last night's blues
in the grey clouds

wedding photographer —
in the air a question
of rain

unswept street —
the bride steps carefully
round last night's garbage

Queen's Pantry,
in its eaves a sparrow
picks at parasites

my cup empty
no excuse to stay
still I linger

searching the sky
for something unnamed
I see only clouds

sparrows scatter —
the thrum of a motorcycle
comes closer

finally sunshine!
the village awakens
to its own music

Midnight Snow

When you walk
through virgin snow
you slide your booted
feet and are surprised
by the grainy sound
that rises above the
wind's song, a kind
of sandpaper friction
in the otherwise quiet
of near midnight…
you look down where
the sidewalk was,
and observe your feet
going where they will.

Only whimsy directs
your steps amongst
the tall shadows cast
by shining street lamps.
In the snow-filled light
arthritic branches become
sidewalk cracks and you
step easily from branch
to branch, a feat
impossible by day,
then you laugh aloud,
a child once more,
your voice dancing
with the midnight snow.

Moonlight Sonata

for Evangeline Bellefontaine and Gabriel Lajeunesse

But Evangeline's heart was sustained by a vision, that faintly
Floated before her eyes, and beckoned her on through the moonlight.
—Henry Wadsworth Longfellow ("Evangeline")

I cannot touch you as the moonlight does:
its fingers slide between us in the dark
that is not darkness, they seep into each pore
and travel where I cannot go, they parody desire
but do not see your lucent countenance drenched
in memories of what must be no more;
only in dreams
can we reconstitute what's gone before,
or in the moon's soft-pedalled afterglow.

Oh that we yet might ride
the boisterous wild arpeggios of dawn
again and yet again and come at last to rest
in some patinaed place, some welcoming grotto
where we would wear our love resplendent
and listen to Zenaida doves all day
and have no need for moonlight.

The Violin Maker

When you found it high
in the Caucasus Mountains
how did you know?

Was it wind or wood
that thrummed unceasing,
beckoning, *sempre passionato,*
sonabile, dolce?

Did you approach it
con amore
knowing that in the taking
something precious
would be lost?

What were you thinking
even as you steadied
the well-honed axe?

Did you say a grateful prayer
in concert with the winter's wind

sotto voce, susurrando, teneramente

offering immortality, promising
a different kind of freedom?

Did you hear four hundred voices
courting the songs of the Caucasus

stringendo, sostenuto, l'istesso

How could you know, frigid, oblivious
to the persistent winds, that this tree
was the one?

Touching Rodin

It is a torso at prayer,
you know that by the slant
of the stilled thighs, the knees
that are bent but unbending,
the way light falls across the dark
surface but does not dance there.
You desire to touch the sacred
moment, to place your fingers
flatly against the mute casting,
to feel its solidity, and imagine
the muscles flexed, their energy
pressing back at you. The idea
is electric, unbearable; you move

closer and note the slight but definite
arch between shoulder blades,
the shadowed hollow still tensed
as if a lover had playfully run
knuckles along the rungs of vertebrae
causing an involuntary response.

It is the arch that holds your gaze,
that hard place where carnal and sacred
meet, as, yielding, you reach out
to touch it.

LEGACIES

Payload

The balance of any day
hangs precariously on the sharp
pivot of what goes into
the dryer between lines
of verse and how always,
cleaning the lint trap distracts
the most purposed mind
even when certain it knows
what you wanted to write

next. It's impossible to hold
that thought unbroken
when the phone rings and
it's obviously the father of your
children calling from away and
all you want — what you need
most is just to write down
your next scrap of vision, but it's

gone, buried between warm lint
and the thunk the phone makes
when you hang hubby up,
as if to say this time the poem
was saved by the proverbial
bell
                    from getting written
and you have to remind
yourself that inspiration will
come again, ignoring the tight
little knot forming in your gut
like an acid hairball
clogging the drain.

It doesn't get any better than this

for Don

Back from servicing it
the hermit eases his tractor
down the road, cleans up
the old hard ridge of snow
left when municipal services
plowed across his driveway,
and smooths a packed path
to the tractor shed.

Suddenly the hermit emits
a boisterous "Yee-Haw!"
then looks round half-hopeful
that someone might have heard;

in the echoing silence he gathers
his new-found strength, carries
feed from the car's cold trunk
to the shed, a large can of gas
to the back porch, and thinks
of all the work he now can do...
moving snow, taking garbage
to the road, removing fallen
branches, an endless list
tantalizing in possibility.

Looking up at a dusking sky
the hermit backs his tractor
cautiously into the shed,
turns it off and awaits
its last susurrant shudder
before he lowers the scoop,
plugs in the block heater

then gently secures the shed,
his weathered hand lingering
an extra moment on the cold
latch, as across the frozen yard
thinning exhaust tendrils
into shadow…

42 Eggs

for Wilfred G. Carter, RCOC-CA

Hard to tell who was more tired
of this war, the old Dutchman or me.

I'd heard the shrill squabble of chickens
when we passed by looking for signs
of the enemy... didn't see any of them,
but oh the racket of those foul birds,
it was like manna to my ears, it made
saliva start to run and from the pit
of my stomach an old ache resurfaced.

Had to try it. Spent the next while
scavenging; it was a fallow time
anyhow with us still waiting for
orders; when the day came
                                                  my buddy and me
hoisted all the old scrap lumber
we could find and took it to the meagre
farm, or what had been one before
the war changed everything;

                                                  the old man
ambled out warily but we could see
in his eyes a fine glint of interest,
no hiding that, or the fact that nights
were still cool.

We made our pitch. Eggs. How many
for the lumber?   It was
hardly lumber, but it would burn and
there was little enough fuel to be had,
and even less money to buy it. He disappeared

into the rough shadows of the house,
came back carrying a dirty, dank sack
held gingerly in thin arms: "I got only 42
but tomorrow they'll lay more, long as…"

his voice trailed off and he looked
in the direction we'd come from, then
back to the wood we'd set down nearby.
It was no mean pile and everything
was barter for all of us now anyhow.
I gestured towards it knowing
no words were necessary to seal the deal,
so we shook hands, and after a short moment
I took the sack carefully, and turned away.

Those eggs would have cost us 75 cents
in local currency, that's 75 cents
for just one egg.

Thoughts on How to Shed a Husband

for B.L.

If you had dreamed the action
you might have noted the similarity —

like peeling a banana
and feeling the sweet sundering

like digging nails into the willing rind
of clementines, breathing deeply
the acrid spurt of juice

like peeling an apple,
the sharp blade separating
skin from flesh…

Did you know that skin and flesh
are not always the same,
not nearly as inseparable
as you'd have thought?

Peeling skin is painful;
cutting flesh wounds forever.

Angrily you want to rip
this husband skin away —
in reality you must take care
to delicately pare
the masculine membrane
(once protector of all you were)
from the underlying flesh,
careful to leave unscarred
the too vulnerable tendrils
of raw nerves, the only proof

of your existence
in this keloid metamorphosis.

In the end
you didn't have
to do a thing —

He simply
left.

Not Spring Cleaning

I'm throwing things out

throwing out
throwing out

throwing
throwing
throwing.

It doesn't matter how
I think or say it
this desire
to throw to rip to tear out
something consumes
even though I can't admit
the object of my anger,
and anger has a way
of fooling you.
Instead
I excavate dark closets
and throw out clothes
which haven't known the warmth
of sunlight, haven't danced
or slithered or just felt good on me
in such a long, forgotten time.

This metaphorical cleansing
does not expunge what
compels me to such wildness
to erase the evidence
of what clings more tenaciously
than silk yet offers
me no relief.

I’ve often wondered why
there were no old dresses
hanging in her closet,
no soft memories left
for me to find
                    after
my mother died.

Palliative for Ash Wednesday

Mother agreed most reluctantly
to my attending my best friend's church
on Ash Wednesday, thought perhaps
it would rub off on me, thought perhaps
I would become enamoured
of the High Anglican mass,
eschew the low.
                                        How silly, I argued,
but still refrained from telling her
the real reason I wanted to go
was so I could walk home
through the slate-grey streets
with a cross of ashes on my forehead.

Without Wings

morning chill
shadow ripples dance
on a leafless tree
    if only I could bring back
    all my dead so easily

softly
a chickadee lights
on an umber bush
    the year my mother died
    the birds never returned

the brook
flows endlessly
over small stones
    this longing for what's gone
    returns over and over

in rotting leaves
a lone chipmunk
nuzzles the ground
    does it search so intently
    for what it already knows?

cold spell
the only moving thing
this cloud my breath makes
    from his sickbed my Dad's voice
    still whispers "This too shall pass"

now I grow old
weighted with dreams
that glisten
    like oil on a duck's feathers
    as if it had no wings at all

Old Recipe Book

Soft,
the pages worn
so silky smooth
each rounded corner
bent, and I
am bending too
to breathe the dust
of fifty years,
grease tinged
smoke spiced
so close am I
to touching
the untouchable;

the book I keep
on darkened shelves,
taking it out rarely
to preserve forever
this essence of
my mother.

Legacy

not even when you sliced
your thumb clear to the bone
on the rusty sickle that was
our lawnmower
                                        then called me
in from play, the tell-tale red
soaking the towel you'd wrapped
around your pain, blood
   still dripping
on the sidewalk, and I so young
asking why, and you so calmly
saying

We have to go to the hospital

even then you never cried out

not till decades later when
the cancer knifed your bones
relentlessly
         and finally I heard
your accumulated pain, felt it
cleave my buffered world
causing even the infant
at my breast to cringe
         her eyes
begging a reassurance
I could not give

Hunting Season
October 2006

Like an old deflating volleyball,
soft on the side where a black dog
tried to work long jaws around it,
the morning moon slips into
the new day with an imagined
hiss; high above pine and oak
and maple, autumn seems not
to touch it.

Amongst birch trees
the voice of one leaf falling.

The sharp reports of distant
guns startle a small flotilla
of mallards near the water's edge
as crimson and orange branches
shudder above them, and I wish
each duck could put on the season's
chameleon colours and disappear
into them   but there is no hiding,

as far away in another country
where hard dirt does not cushion falls,
where birds sing while gunfire thunders
and ideology crashes
into reality,
there is no camouflage
for soldier number forty.*

*Trooper Mark Wilson, 39, killed in Afghanistan October 7, 2006

"An Unfortunate Accident"

Solemn, resolute, their commander
speaks into the anxious silence
at the faces looking for answers,
and if not answers, for meaning:

"We look at this as an unfortunate accident..."

Images present of toddlers
falling down stairs,
of the newly licensed rear-
ending the car in front,
of turning my ankle on
a street in Ottawa and ending
up on crutches, of breaking
my fingernail trying to open
a package of California
raspberries, of biting a crouton
and losing a filling just before
the New Year's party —
                                        all of these
are unfortunate, and
accidental.

I do not think when a jeep
in Afghanistan drives over
a bomb planted by insurgents
that *that* is an accident.

Nor can I believe the vileness
of soldiers against an invisible
terror justifies the labeling
of such a loss, unfortunate.

Some one planted that bomb
with intent and that intent
bore fruit, the fruit of dismantled
limbs, of torsos
                        ripped apart
now lifeless, now only ragged
pieces of what was once human —

three soldiers, the untimely victims
of a cruel accident, and oh…
how brutally unfortunate.

At the Cenotaph

Birch roots rise out of chill November ground, become trunk which then cleaves itself; two white tangents mirror each to each, reach up, change their minds and splice together again a leg's length above, wrapping around one another, lovers entwined; now solidly side-by-side they twist together like candy cane stripes (you could walk around them, wonder where they began, where they might end); cloven, they nestle so closely they might be deemed one again, the birch tree doing its slow tango, so slow movement is intuited not seen, yet in its meiotic clasp the suggestion of desire forever linked to genesis ... while in the background a lone bugle trumps the Last Post
for all who have gone before.

Pierre Elliott Trudeau (1919-2000)

Enigma! I voted for
your charisma — thought
you young though my father's age

failed to see the contradiction

captivated by your steel-like
gaze and rolled-up sleeves
                                        seduced
by the energy radiating from
our old black and white TV:

only years later would I decry
your legacy, whose infancy
swayed my first vote
                    still
there is a place where
like an old lover
I accord you
grudging respect.

The Cocktail Hour

he speaks to me of civilization
and how it has advanced

to where

we no longer kill
for want of a loaf of bread
as in former times

no longer imprison
children in workhouses
citing Dickens

no longer castrate
when two people love
citing Héloise and Abelard

and I can't stop my wandering
mind, can't face the smugness
in his eyes as I remember

the latest figures that make
children into statistics

in other countries

pictures from television
of children working
fields and factories
or just scavenging

in other countries

the face
of a woman who
may yet be stoned
for having a child
out of wedlock

in another country

over the clink of ice
the insouciant murmur and coo
of talking   not hearing

I ask
where this line
that divides ours

from other countries
might be

This shape, unstooped

Bones! Listen up!
I have a need to know why,
why you are so silent
about your business, moving
carrying, lifting this mass

of skin and muscle and blood,
of neurons and hair, those
silken ones that stand sentinel
over all this ragged body…
I need you to spill
your secrets, give definition
to tales revealed by nosey, whirring
machines, tales of density or lack
of it, of lacey intricacies where once
hard bone held me erect, of intimate
pictures of ball leaning into socket,
and vertebrae spooning vertebrae,
now become skeletal maps requiring
a skilled technician to translate.

Tell me if what's missing
is only bone. When Samson
lost his hair he lost his strength.

It's my bones I wish to hear before
the rattle comes. I'm listening
for their phosphorescent whisper —

Bones! Hear me now   feel
the weight of me
hang warm around you
and remember, I have a fondness
for this shape, unstooped.

Full Circle

It starts slowly, a small twinge
and you wonder if this is it
if it could possibly be this easy
the germ of an idea from so many
months ago, a kind of cerebral knowing,
you *thought* baby but didn't feel it,
waited for the seed to grow, felt
like a farmer who daily watches his field
(the insistent crows circling)
who smells the air, looking for rain

and not until the first drop would it seem
real, that one tremulous globule of water
presaging more
the farmer
imagines the soft kernel of seed expand,
explode into life
                                it seems
forever before you feel it, that slight
primeval flutter: you still wonder
if it will happen, question your own
integrity even as pain brings you back
to your ponderous abdomen, tight
like an overblown balloon, and you ride
its crest to an urgency not of *your* making.

Between breaths you imagine it
a separate entity, of you but not you,
if it ever was.

White Star Line

R.M.S. Regina, 1927

In the photograph
my grandmother still
wondering why
why he would leave behind
everything, home and
the unkempt piece of grass
which hid the memory
of the child who died,
how she would manage
on foreign soil
friendless and alone
with such a brood
to feed, to clothe,
to tell why
this wild decision.

In front of her, seven
children stare bravely
into a future they can
only imagine; the tallest
a smiling boy of fourteen,
the youngest a toddler
in his mother's arms.
My mother wears her
Brownie uniform severely,
the knotted tie pushing
against her chin —
her best dress-up clothes.

The moment speaks
of smiles frozen in time,
of silent hopes and fears,

and I am mute
trying to read
the black and white
image, knowing
how history rewrote
their dream
                    wondering
if she would have thought it
worth the while.

The Meanest Flower That Blows

the immigrants, two years later

The dancing flowers remain
anonymous; what is known
is what is seen, an amiable
beauty. One might swear
they keep their determined watch
lest some spirited beings cast
a jealous spell upon the smiling
family.

The mother holds her son close
as mothers do, this boy born
into a land not of prickly gorse
and idle ironworks, but of promise
sown into turned earth, of wind-
burned skin and calloused hands.

This day the breeze is gentle,
the daisy-like flowers amenable,
and hope swells with each nod
of their sun-warmed heads

the flowers dance
a child and his parents
smile for the camera

Author's Notes

"Walking the Eston Hills for the First Time" — Between 1850 and 1949 the ironstone mines in Eston, my mother's birthplace in North Yorkshire, yielded over 63,000,000 tons of the ore, and, by 1874, Great Britain was producing about half the world's total of pig iron, according to historian Maurice E. Wilson in *The Story of Eston*. Wilson observes that by 1880 what had once been pastoral countryside had become "a flaming patchwork of blast furnaces," noting also that in 1883, Eston Mine alone produced 1,372,778 tons of ironstone. After WWI, Eston and the surrounding area fell upon hard times as demand for iron and steel declined sharply and the entire country slid toward the Depression years. Unemployment grew, and it was during this difficult time that my grandparents and their then seven children emigrated to Canada.

Cnaep/Nab is a Saxon word indicating the summit of a hill.

"Geographies" — Frisia is a historic coastal region of the Netherlands and Germany, along the southeastern edge of the North Sea. Saltburn-by-the-Sea is a town on the northeast coast of England, in North Yorkshire.

"Toogood Pond" — *Chupa* is a canopy beneath which Jewish marriage ceremonies are performed, often consisting of greenery and flowers. *Selah*, found throughout the Bible, is a kind of verbal rest, allowing the reader to pause and consider.

"Kaddish" — My own non-Jewish understanding of *Kaddish* is that it lies somewhere between a prayer and a blessing, and this is how I have used it, as a title, in the "Kaddish" section of *small flames*.

"After the Music" was written the morning after the Markham Jazz Festival in 2006. In the same year it placed in the Bulgarian International Haiku contest "Haiku and Musik," and I read part of the sequence on Bulgarian National Radio's *The Zone of Rock and Jazz*, with simultaneous translation.

"The Violin Maker" — from an article in *The Toronto Star*, May 14, 2005, "From tree to timbre." In the winter of 1967, 1300 metres up in the Caucasus Mountains, Hratch Armenious Tchalkouchian and some friends cut down an Armenian maple. It took four days to lug it down the mountainside. As a luthier, over the next 40 years, he has made nearly 400 violins from that tree, and was still doing so at the time of the article. Armenious violins are coveted round the world.

"42 Eggs" — The story on which this poem is based was told in a letter from somewhere in Europe, sent by my Uncle Miff Carter to his sister, my mother, April 7, 1945.

Acknowledgements

Some of the poems in this book, or earlier versions of them, first appeared in the following: *Arts in Motion: Newsletter of the Markham Arts Council, Ash Moon Anthology: Poems on Aging in Modern English Tanka, contemporary verse 2, Handprints on the Future, Outreach Connection, Oval Victory: The Best of Canadian Poetry, People's Poetry Letter, The Antigonish Review, The Cormorant, The Gaspereau Review, The Zone of Rock and Jazz,* Bulgarian National Radio, *Windfall, Words Dance.*

Heartfelt thanks goes first of all to my family: my husband Dave, and my adult children Pamela, Andrea, David and Elizabeth, for their unflagging support, and for believing in me always.

My sincere gratitude to Karen Haughian, publisher of Signature Editions, for making my book real.

Special thanks goes to George Payerle, my gentle editor from Signature Editions, for his endless patience and his inspired insights. My thanks also to Allan Briesmaster, who was instrumental in the first shaping and editing of *small flames.*

Further thanks go to Anne Simpson and Robyn Sarah and the amazing poets with whom I shared the 2003 and 2005 Maritime Writers' Workshops at UNB, for all their support and encouragement; also to Bernice Lever, to David Helwig, and to the late poet Joseph Sherman, who was both mentor and encourager in the earliest days of my manuscript.

Special thanks also to Jeremy Relph for sharing both his time, and his experiences in Afghanistan.

About the Author

Dina E. Cox is a writer and musician, and now an empty nester, living with her husband, David, in a northern suburb of Toronto; several children, and a Biblical number of grandchildren, live near enough for frequent visits. Dina was born to parents of straitened means in postwar Saint John, N.B., but the family's fortunes improved and she went on to the University of New Brunswick, then taught high school in the province before marrying. As a B.A. English (Hons.) and neophyte writer she devoted herself to her husband and children, not returning to her pen until they were all grown.

Dina Cox's poems have appeared in periodicals as diverse as *The Antigonish Review, tempslibre, The Cormorant, CV2, Room* and *Simply Haiku,* and have been published in Canada, the U.S., Ireland, and Bulgaria. She has also won numerous awards, including the Betty Drevniok Award from Haiku Canada, the nation's premier award for English language poetry in that form. *small flames* is her first book.